What Sha

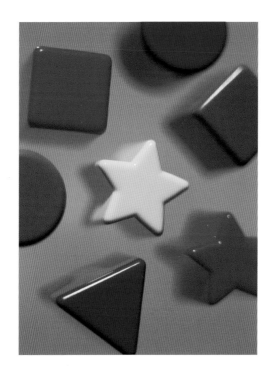

written by Pam Holden

1

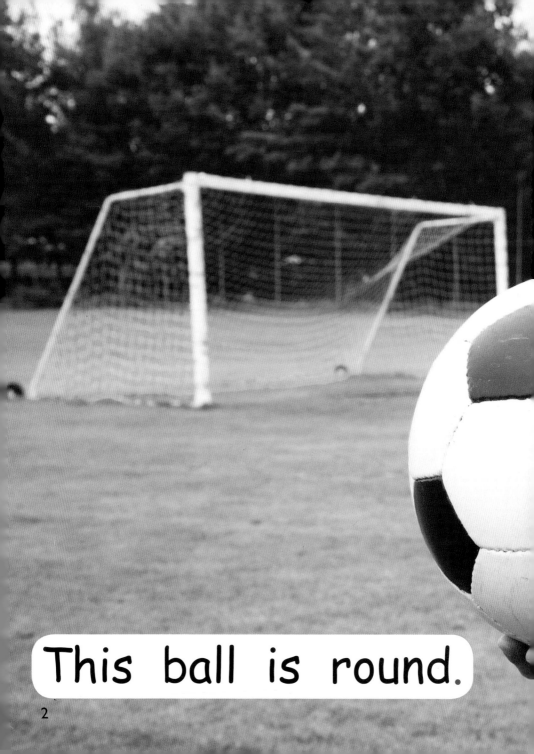

This ball is round.

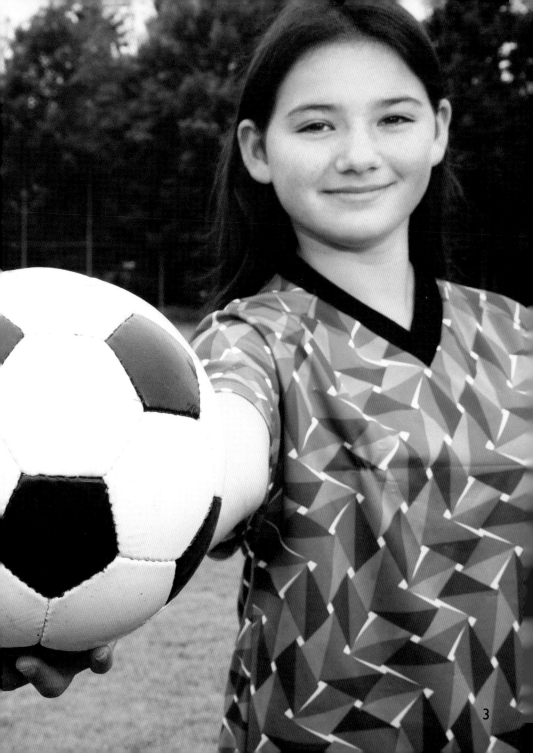

This book is
a rectangle.

What Feels Cold?

written by Pam Holden

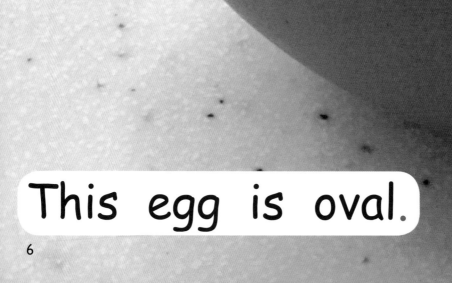

This egg is oval.

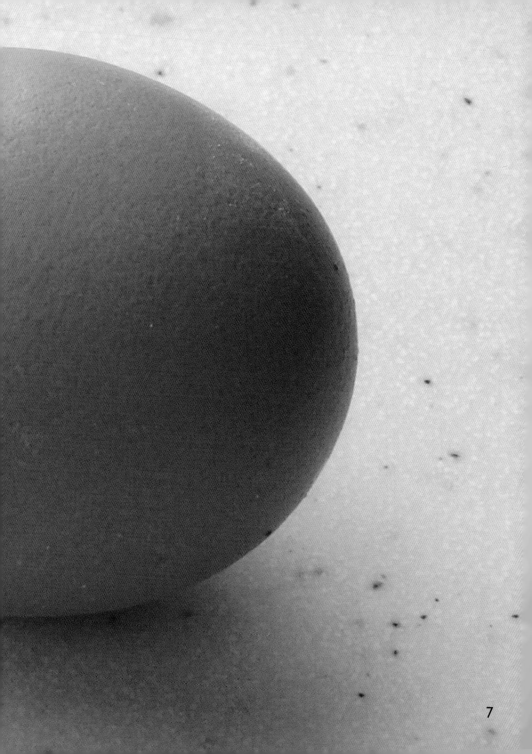

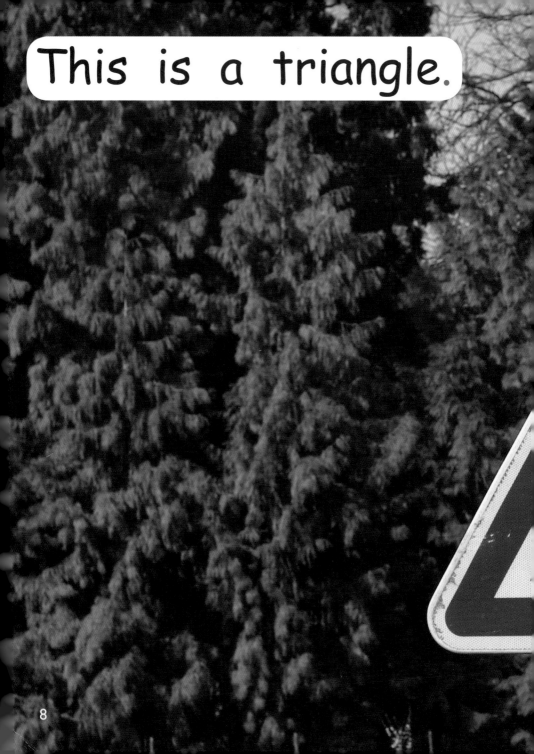

This is a triangle.

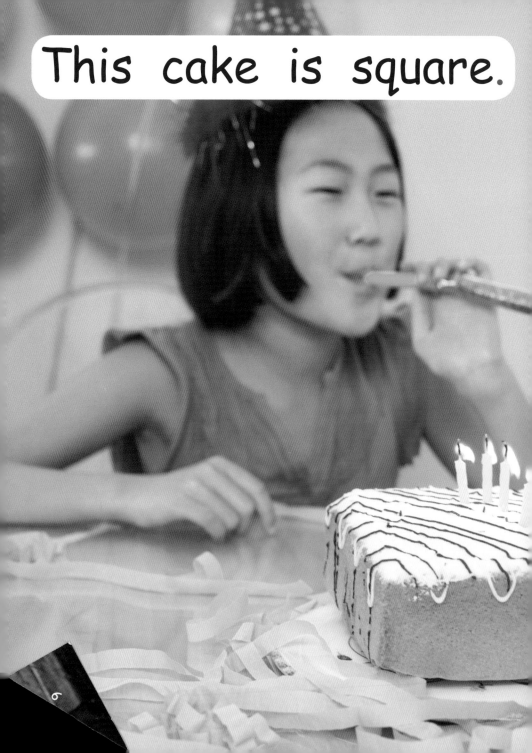

This cake is square.

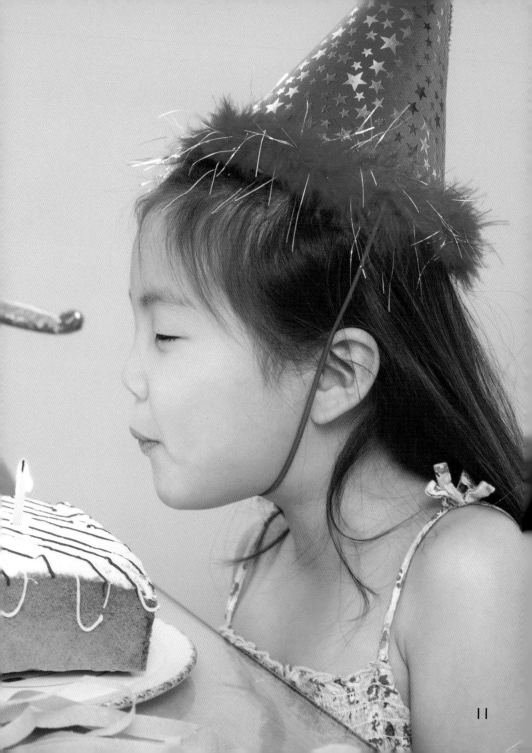

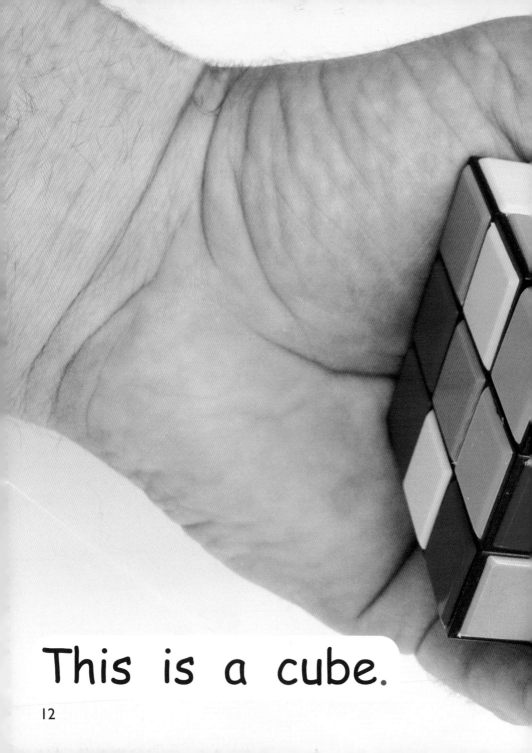

This is a cube.

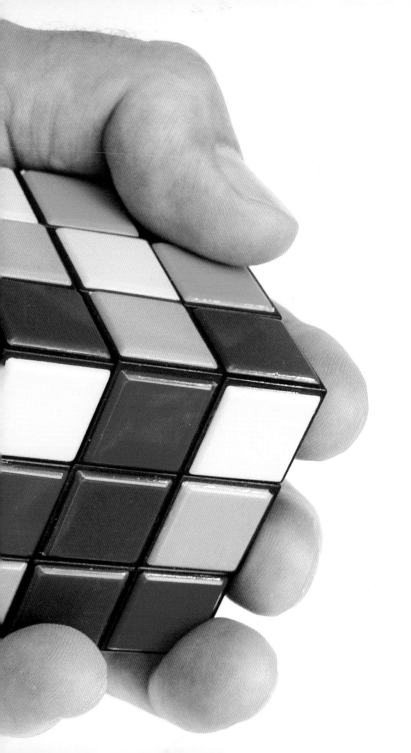

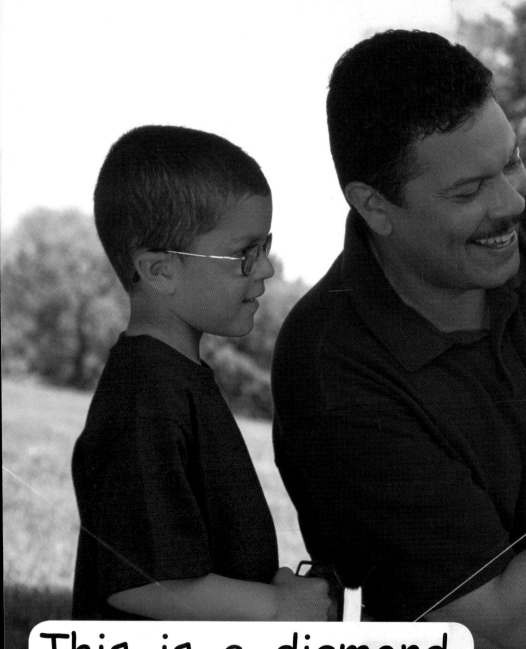

This is a diamond.

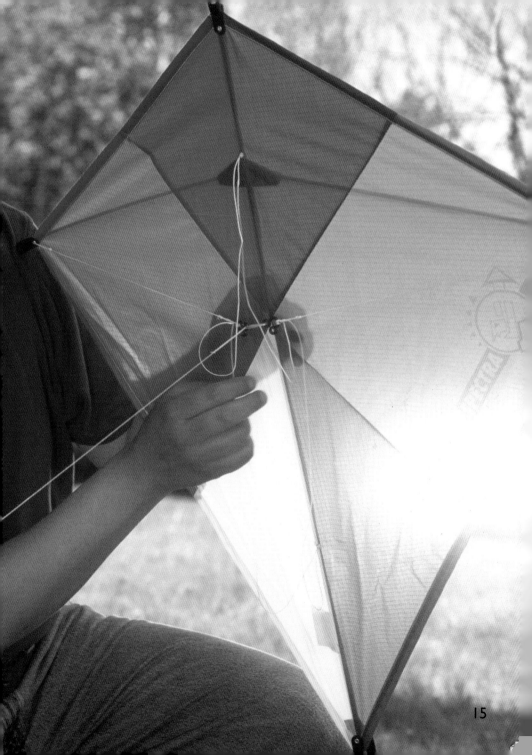

This is a star.
Twinkle, twinkle!

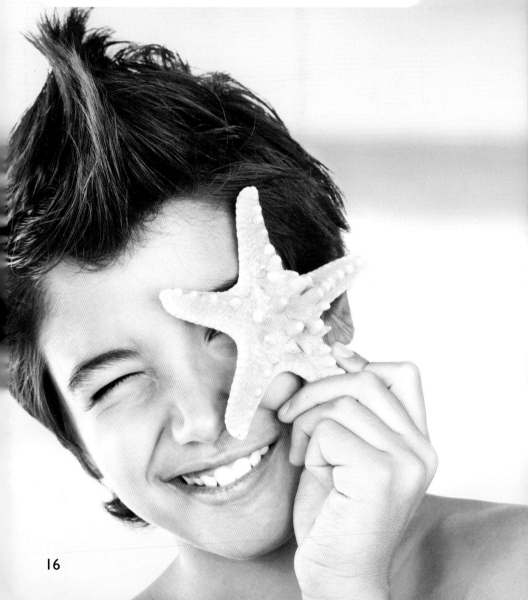